Life Cycles

CHICKENS

Julie K. Lundgren

ROURKE PUBLISHING

www.rourkepublishing.com

www.rourkepublishing.com

Project Assistance:
The author thanks Jane Boerboom for chicken advice, and Blue Door Publishing.

Photo credits: Cover © Roger Browning, Rudyanto Wijaya, Margo Harrison, Fortish; Title Page © Fortish; Contents © Petrina, Coprid, cameilia; Page 5 © joyfuldesigns, Marina Ivanova; Page 6 © Boykov; Page 7 © Sveta San; Page 8 © S.Cooper Digital; Page 9 © Stephan Westcott; Page 10 © Gmoose1; Page 11 © Carolina K. Smith, M.D.; Page 12 © Marsha Goldenberg; Page 13 © Petr Jilek; Page 14 © saied shahin kiya; Page 15 © Adi, cameilia; Page 16 © cameilia; Page 17 © Martin Kucera; Page 18 © Eric Isselée; Page 19 © photosbyjohn; Page 20 © Lee O'Dell; Page 21 © nikkytok; Page 22 © Gmoose1, saied shahin kiya, manzrussali, Petrina

Editor: Jeanne Sturm

Cover and page design by Nicola Stratford, bdpublishing.com

Library of Congress Cataloging-in-Publication Data

Lundgren, Julie K.
 Chickens / Julie K. Lundgren.
    p. cm. -- (Life cycles)
 Includes bibliographical references and index.
 ISBN 978-1-61590-311-5 (Hard cover) (alk. paper)
 ISBN 978-1-61590-550-8 (Soft cover)
 1. Chickens--Juvenile literature. I. Title.
 SF487.5.L86 2011
 636.5--dc22
                            2010009028

Rourke Publishing
Printed in the United States of America, North Mankato, Minnesota
033010
033010LP

www.rourkepublishing.com - rourke@rourkepublishing.com
Post Office Box 643328, Vero Beach, Florida 32964

Table of Contents

Useful Birds

Chickens are some of the world's most common birds. Like other birds, they have beaks, feathers, and wings. Even with wings, most chickens cannot fly. Instead, their wings act like booster rockets as they run along the ground or jump over a fence.

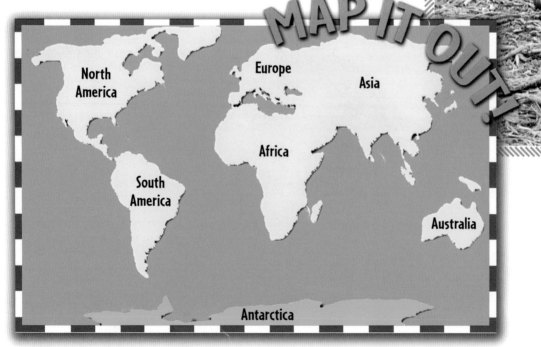

MAP IT OUT!

North America

Europe

Asia

Africa

South America

Australia

Antarctica

Domestic chickens live all over the world, except on Antarctica.

Chickens first became tame, or **domestic**, birds at least 4,000 years ago in Southeast Asia. They developed from a kind of wild bird called the red jungle fowl.

Wild red jungle fowl still live in Asia.

Farmers often feed kitchen scraps to their flocks. Many chickens love juicy watermelon rinds and fresh corncobs.

Farmers raise chickens for their meat and eggs. Small **flocks** often roam free. These chickens scratch in the dirt for seeds, grass, worms, insects, and berries. They also help control pests that could harm the farmers' crops.

Large farms raise thousands of chickens at once.

Chickens on large farms grow in pens and eat special feed made of grains and vitamins.

A Dutch bantam has a big, red comb on top of his head.

Over the years, people have developed many kinds of chickens. Different **breeds** have differences in size, color, types of feathers, and **comb** shape.

Many people enjoy showing their chickens at fairs and chicken shows. They win ribbons and the honor of owning the best chicken of its breed. Still others enjoy chickens as pets.

Some breeds have fine, silken feathers, like the silkie bantam.

More than 280 million chickens live in the United States.

First, The Egg

All life begins, grows, **reproduces**, and dies. This life cycle repeats without end. The chicken life cycle starts when a female, or hen, lays an egg. Only eggs **fertilized** by a male chicken, or rooster, will make chicks.

Not all chicken eggs are white. Different breeds lay different colors of eggs. Eggs can be brown, blue, tan, or green.

Buff Orpington hens lay light brown eggs.

A hen lays one egg each day until she has a **clutch** of several eggs. She settles gently on the eggs to warm them. Every so often, she turns them with her beak to warm the other side.

Many animals, like foxes, steal
and eat chickens and their eggs.

At night, chickens are kept safely in a barn or pen. They often roost up high to sleep. To protect their eggs, they lay them in a nest box or hide them.

Inside the egg, the egg white provides protection and nutrition to the chick. The chick forms in the yolk. The yolk provides the chick's main food. The hard shell protects the chick.

INSIDE THE EGG

egg shell

egg white

egg yolk

The chick forms in the yolk.

air

DID YOU KNOW?

Bird eggs have hard shells with thousands of very tiny holes that allow fresh air to pass through.

The chick may take a full day to free itself from its shell.

Cool Chicks

The chick rests while its down dries.

Eggs hatch in about 21 days. First, sounds of tapping and peeping come from the egg. The chick uses a sharp bump on its beak called the **egg tooth** to chip and hammer its way out of the shell. Later, the egg tooth falls off.

Chicks come out wet and tired. Their delicate **down** feathers dry quickly and fluff out. They eat what adult chickens eat.

Newly hatched chicks can walk.

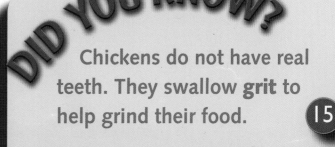

DID YOU KNOW?

Chickens do not have real teeth. They swallow **grit** to help grind their food.

15

Unlike other animals that lay eggs, like snakes and turtles, chickens care for their young. The hen keeps her chicks warm and safe.

A curious chick explores the world with its eyes, ears, and beak.

Hens can tell the peeps of their chicks from the peeps of other hens' chicks.

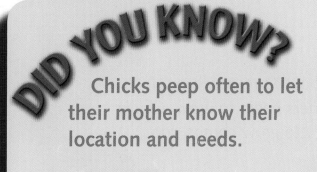

DID YOU KNOW?

Chicks peep often to let their mother know their location and needs.

People can raise chicks without a hen, too. They order chicks or fertilized eggs through the mail, at a farm store, or at a nearby farm. They provide food, water, and a warm, safe place to grow.

In about four weeks, adult feathers begin to grow. Chicks begin to grow combs, too.

These chicks keep warm under a heat lamp.

Cycle Snapshot

Chicks grow into adult chickens in about six months. Chickens can live 10 to 15 years.

Hens and Roosters

Hens begin to lay eggs when they are six months old. Roosters can partner with many hens to fertilize the eggs. People collect unfertilized eggs for eating or selling to a market or store.

Roosters crow to warn the flock of danger and defend their homes. They will fight to protect their hens.

A hen can lay 250 to 300 eggs each year. Most of the eggs are packed and sold for people to eat.

City Chickens

More cities are becoming chicken friendly. Laws in many cities allow people to keep one or more hens. Sometimes chicken owners are required to get permission from their neighbors. Roosters crow loudly and often, so they still need country homes.

21

Life Cycle Round-up

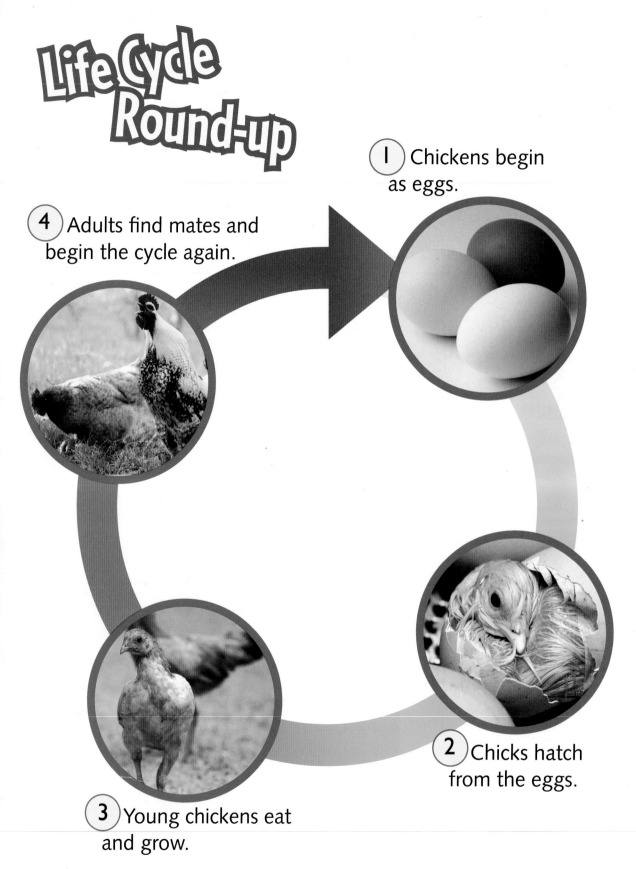

1 Chickens begin as eggs.

4 Adults find mates and begin the cycle again.

2 Chicks hatch from the eggs.

3 Young chickens eat and grow.

Glossary

breeds (BREEDZ): different kinds of a type of animal, like dog breeds

clutch (KLUHCH): a group of eggs from one hen that are laid within a few days of each other

comb (KOHM): the thick flap of skin on top of a chicken's head that comes in different shapes, colors, and sizes depending on the breed

domestic (duh-MESS-tik): no longer wild; like farm animals and housecats

down (DOWN): light, fluffy, warm feathers

egg tooth (EG TOOTH): a sharp, hard point on a chick's beak, used to crack the shell during hatching

fertilized (FUR-tuh-lized): joined with the rooster's seed, or sperm, so a chick will grow

flocks (FLOKS): groups of birds that stay together throughout their daily activities

grit (GRIT): small pebbles and sand swallowed by some birds to aid digestion

reproduces (ree-pruh-DOOSS-ehz): makes more of something

Index

Websites to Visit

http://gets.gc.k12.va.us/elementary/lifecycles/chickens.htm

www.albc-usa.org/cpl/wtchlist.html#chickens

www.vtaide.com/png/chicken.htm

www.incredibleegg.org

www.mypetchicken.com/default.aspx

www.kiddyhouse.com/Farm/Chicken/Chicken.html

About the Author

Julie K. Lundgren grew up near Lake Superior where she reveled in mucking about in the woods, picking berries, and expanding her rock collection. Her appetite for learning about nature led her to a degree in biology from the University of Minnesota. She currently lives in Minnesota with her husband and two sons.